How to Make Money on Triller: A Beginner's Guide to Earning Mad Cash

Lisa Reinke

There is no guarantee that you will earn any money using the techniques and ideas in these materials. Examples in these materials are not to be interpreted as a promise or guarantee of earnings. Earning potential is entirely dependent on the person using our product, ideas, and techniques. We do not purport this as a get rich scheme. Your level of success in attaining the results claimed in our materials depends on the time you devote, ideas and techniques mentioned, your finances, knowledge and various skills. Since these factors differ according to individuals, we cannot guarantee your success or income level. Nor are we responsible for any of your actions. Materials in our product may contain information that includes or is based upon forward-looking statements within the meaning of the securities litigation reform act of 1995. Forward-looking statements give our expectations or forecasts of future events. You can identify these statements by the fact that they do not relate strictly to historical or current facts. They use words such as "anticipate," "estimate," "expect,"

Cover photo licensed 9/11/20 with purchase #192711422 by user
ID 40193562 Lisa Reinke through:
Depositphotos Inc.
Address: 115 West 30th Street, Suite 1110B, New York, NY,
10001, United States
E-mail: support@depositphotos.com
Website: www.depositphotos.com
Phone: +1-954-990-0075 Photo copyright held by Yaping Ma.

Contact the author at author@cheerful.com

ISBN: 9798685719676
Imprint: Independently published

CONTENTS

INTRODUCTION

Despite your occupation in this modern world, it is vital for everyone to be familiar with various social media platforms. Not being familiar with these spaces means you are not on equal footing with others and, therefore, at a disadvantage. With time, these spaces have grown to become virtual communities and have become places of work for countless of the users. From Youtubers making videos designed to entertain the masses to Instagram posts made to flaunt your lifestyle, people are earning 'mad cash' on social media.

Triller is one of these platforms that has only recently been brought to the limelight after years of improvement and upgrades. Similar to TikTok, the platform provides people the opportunity to gather a following by posting 15-second-long video content on the application. Seeing the TikTok stars rise to fame so quickly, every user is looking for the perfect formula to earn heaps of cash and live an extravagant lifestyle like them. The following book directs average users through the various opportunities available to earn money on Triller. It assists the reader in understanding the process and cautions them of any mishaps that can occur when employing each of the methods discussed.

So, read attentively to prepare yourself to milk the cow that Triller is.

TRILLER 101: INTRODUCTION TO TRILLER

This generation is defined by its rapid technological transformations and advancements, which has caused our online behavior to alter significantly. Our presence online has shifted from emails to social media, and this pattern has increased exponentially in the past decade. The ability of social media to connect us with people and to allow us to share our lives with them has become a part of our daily life and a constant source of entertainment. Applications like Facebook, Twitter, YouTube, and Instagram have become a part of our daily routine, and we spend many hours everyday surfing these applications.

TikTok is one of the apps that made its marks by attracting users over a period of almost four years. In early 2020, the Chinese application had over 2 billion downloads and was the favorite application of every child and young adult globally. With its rise to popularity, the application drew added eyes for scrutiny. It was involved in a conspiracy because its rumored to have an affiliation with the Chinese government and to be leaking users' personal data. Since then, many countries, including the United States of America, Australia, and the United Kingdom, have expressed their concerns over the application. Some countries like India have made the aggressive move to ban the application completely. This is the reason why many users started moving to an alternative application called Triller. Many TikTok famed personalities like Josh Richards, Bryce Hall, Noah Beck, and Griffin Johnson have moved to the application, urging their almost 50 million combined followers to do the same.

In 2020, Triller was able to dethrone TikTok from its number one position on the App Store and has been continuing to attract personalities like Donald Trump, Chance the Rapper, and Snoop Dogg to join and support their platform. So, what exactly is Triller, and how is it better from TikTok?

What is Triller?

Introduced in 2015 by app developers Sammy Rubin and David Leiberman, Triller was initially launched as a video editing application powered by artificial intelligence to ease a user's experience. This meant that users would be able to film themselves, and the application enabled the user's option to multiple takes. Later, the application's artificial intelligence would automatically cut, edit, and compile the best takes together for the user in a singular video. Since then, the application has altered its user interface (UI) and turned it into a social media application where 15-second clips can be posted by the user to be watched by others on the platform. Similar to TikTok and other social applications, these published clips can be liked, commented on, and shared by other users. Users can also make use of the in-app tools including, filters, drawings, and music.

As this book is being written, Triller has been downloaded more than 250 million times and leads the App Store in more than 50 markets. If one is aware of TikTok and is a user of the application, navigating Triller will not be difficult at all. The application follows the same interface as TikTok and is friendly to the users who are new on the platform. The outlay of Triller is also very similar to TikTok with a Home page and a Discover section.

The Home page of Triller comprises the following section: Following, Music, and Social. The Music and Social areas of this feature have striking similarities to the For You page of TikTok. This is the section where one can find all the trending videos and the latest trends that have been circulating on the platform. The Discover section, which is symbolized in a music symbol on the navigation bar, is a place for users to find new music. Once a user finds a track that they like, they can play the entire track, use them in their Triller videos, or even look up popular videos circulating on the application that uses the same track.

With so many striking similarities to TikTok and a mass of people switching to Triller, certain features make it stand out from the Chinese-run application. These reasons are discussed below.

TikTok vs. Triller

Despite similar outlay, operations, and features, Triller is, in many ways, different from TikTok. For starters, music is very integral for Triller and distinguishes it from its counterpart. The Chinese-run application is working against the already established music empires, whereas Triller collaborates with them. It is rumored that TikTok plans to start its own streaming service, which can be a threat to already established businesses in the sector. Moreover, a user can only listen to 15 seconds of a track on TikTok and can only use the songs available on the application and therefore users are limited in terms of choice. On the other hand, Triller has dealt with many major labels, including, but not limited to, Warner Brother Records, Sony Music, and Atlantic Records. These deals allow users to stream, not just 15 seconds, but also the entire track on Triller and use music to make Triller from their personal music libraries on Spotify and Apple Music.

Secondly, both the applications use their artificial intelligence to serve the users in a very different and unique manner. TikTok uses the AI to give the application the ability to serve the user's suggestions that are customized to their liking by taking into account their search history. Their viewing history and the following are also taken into account to present them with an assortment of content that they will like. However, Triller uses AI technology in capacities involving video alteration. As stated before, it edits videos for the users automatically.

Additionally, the algorithm on both applications is also designed differently. TikTok has grown a name for allowing people to acquire fame easily compared to other social media applications like Instagram and YouTube because the application's algorithm shows videos to the user based on the trending nature and intriguing content. The Triller algorithm, on the contrary, is designed to favor artist accounts.

I hope this was enough to introduce you to Triller and point out the fundamental differences between the competing application, TikTok. However, we have seen many TikTok 'stars' rise to fame and earn piles of money at very young ages. A popular name you might be aware of is Charlie D'Amelio, who is only 16 years old. Making money on such platforms is possible, and if one has a decent following, it can be easy. The following chapters will explore how an average user can start generating 'mad cash' on Triller.

ONLY ON TRILLER

With every passing day, Triller is getting more people to sign up on its platform by introducing security measures, innovative features, and monetization methods. People have started to realize the real value and opportunities that lie within the social media sphere and are starting to cash in on them. Every teenager who is now joining these applications is doing so with the motive to either gain fame, money, or both. In a world before the introduction of TikTok, this seemed very difficult. YouTube is a prime example of it, where content mattered and was time-consuming to produce. Many people dedicated years without success to build followership and eventually gave up on their dreams, while some, despite many hurdles, continue to excel. With TikTok's unique algorithm earning fame became comparatively easier, and this pattern is also followed in Triller. Making money on these applications requires a following, and depending on the number of followers one has, the zeros in the earnings check of the creators will be decided. Apart from conventional means, which have become common knowledge to generate money (which we will explore later in the book), Triller has started a monetization platform for its creators. How this feature works and what it is, is described below.

Triller 7.0

The LA-based social media application, Triller, allows fans to raise funds for 'purpose-driven goals' by introducing a monetization platform called Triller 7.0. This platform will enable fans, brands, and music labels to donate to the influencers to achieve their goals. The scope of these goals can extend from college tuition fees to raising money for new equipment. The range of goals for which money can be raised is vast, as the requirements are loose enough for anyone to structure their goals around them. This platform can be equated to Kickstarter, as the purpose of this platform is also to allow creators to gather crowdfunding for their goals. This platform aims to allow the users an opportunity to have a chance at achieving their dreams, and the CEO of the application believes that this platform helps make it possible. Right now, Triller 7.0 is only accessible to certain people to raise funds and functions on an invitation-only basis. Despite this exclusivity of a French influencer, Lea Elui was one of the first to have an opportunity to take advantage of this feature. She created four videos over the course of three days to spread the word around for her 'purpose-driven goal' of gathering money to fund her college tuition. She raised 50,000 United States dollars (USD) from over 3000 supporters in this very brief period. Her story shows the promising success of this platform and the extent of wonders it could do for creators. By the time you are reading this, Triller may have opened up the gates to this method for you.

Donations

Another feature that is only accessible on the Triller platform is the ability for fans, music labels, and brands to donate money to their creators solely because they like their content. Triller says that this feature gives its creators the sole ownership and control over the kind of content they want to produce by introducing monetization, and eliminating the need to rely on external product promotions to impact their content. Moreover, some of the other platforms restrict donations only from the creator's fan-base. Still, taking advantage of their strong relations with the music industry, Triller has allowed labels to donate to artists. This means that rising musicians can sell their craft on the platform, earn appreciation, and probably a record deal from the labels as the record labels are scouting them. However, the application only adds the 'Donate' button to verified accounts. Like most of the other applications, verification depends on the popularity of the creators, and on their followers.

The Triller platform has its own currency called Gold and Gems. Once the 'Donate' button appears on a creator's profile, other users can convert the real cash to buy Triller Gold. The Triller Wallet is where users can keep count of the money and manage their virtual cash. The Triller Gold currency can be donated to verified users, and the creators can convert their donated Gold into Gem, which can be later converted to real cash. It is important to note that only Gems can be converted back into real money, and total cash can only be converted into Gold. These features enable people to monetize their content and promote their original music, dance videos, or any other content. This feature also serves as a motivation for creators to continue doing what they want to do.

MERCHANDISE AND PAID PROMOTIONS

With increasing followers, likes, and regular content, one grows a name for themselves on social media platforms. The more popular you are, the more doors will be opened for you to generate money. The following that one creates is loyal to the user and grows a fondness for them. This means that any product you promote, be it yours or anyone else's, can be reached to masses and will be bought by many out of love for the creator. Keeping this in mind, and the massive audience that social media stars can reach, many companies pay them to promote their service or their product. This trend is common on Facebook, Instagram, YouTube, and TikTok.

Similarly, it is also not uncommon for creators to develop their own products to market to their audience. Merchandise is very popular amongst the social media community of creators. Fans are always on a lookout for any piece of clothing, jewelry, or any other accessory that they can own to show off their love for the creator and support them. For most of the prominent creators, paid promotions and merchandise is their primary source of earning. Some of the popular influencers that you might be aware of are Mr. Beast and David Dobrik.

The following delves into detail on how to design, market, and sell your merchandise on Triller and also how to get paid promotions and negotiate the terms.

Merchandise

Once you set up an account on any of the social media websites and achieve a following, you start the process of branding yourself. Regardless of whether you are mindful of this fact, the account name, content, and the fan-base are factors that define and create a specific brand for you. Most of the following you generate is attracted to this branding, and these people will only stick with you if they continue to be entertained by the brand. However, views and follows can restrict the realm of monetization, and often it can be quite insignificant. One of the ways to spread the boundaries of monetization is influencer merchandise that not only brings money, but also promotes your brand.

Merchandise is an easy and great way to earn money and to engage with your audience if you have a loyal and engaging community of fans. Although having a huge following is a reliable indicator of the success of your social media presence, selling merch would not be lucrative unless your audience is engaged. This means that there is a constant stream of comments and likes on your videos and an active effort from you to engage with your followers. It is essential that you listen to your followers when you make the decision to sell the merch. Is your fan-base strong enough for you to release merch? What should be the design of your merch? What should be the type of clothing or accessory that will be liked by your followers? These are some of the questions you need to ask yourself before releasing influencer merch. As long as the merchandise is stylish, comfortable, and has inclusive sizes, it will do well.

To design the merchandise, stick to your branding because it is not just a means of earning, but also something that you are giving to your followers. It has to be trendy and comfortable so the fans can wear and flaunt it, in order to support you and spread your brand. The design should encompass your persona on Triller. It can be something you say a lot, a running joke on your account, or something that the fans relate you with. David Dobrik is known for his clickbait titles and thumbnails and therefore uses the term 'Clickbait' on his merchandise. Unlike most platforms, Triller has also launched an easy to design program that allows creators to design and customize their merch as per their own taste, thus making the entire process less stressful and more manageable. The platform also has an affiliation with manufacturers and merchants to assist creators from the beginning to the end of the process of creating and selling merch. Such resources are not provided by most of the platforms, but Triller relieves their influencers from most of the burden that comes from releasing merchandise. Keep in mind that hoodies, T-shirts, and caps are some of the most popular merchandise items amongst fans.

Once you have designed your merchandise, shamelessly promote it on Triller and release any relevant information to your fans about the merch. Do not just restrict yourself to Triller while promoting it, but rather do it on other platforms also, as you are likely to attract some traffic on different mediums. You can do merchandise reveal content, giveaways, discount codes, and release limited merchandise to generate more excitement and boost sales. Lastly, always be mindful of the quantity of merchandise you produce and have in-stock. Always produce an amount that you think you can sell, rather than producing in excess and incurring losses. You can always produce more but not get rid of what has been manufactured already.

If you keep these tips in mind and are liked by your followers on Triller, you will surely do well and ultimately sell out the merch.

Paid Promotions

It is not surprising that social media influencers can afford the most expensive lifestyle since paid promotions can alone pay them thousands of dollars per post. It is rumored that Kim Kardashian bags $300,000 to $500,000 for a single Instagram post. Paid promotions can be one of the most significant revenue streams for online personalities. Like merchandise, branding also plays a very significant role for one to acquire a brand deal. This will define your niche and attract respective brands and products to approach you and give you brand deals. A person who is regularly posting about food will get food-related sponsorships, while a fitness content creator will receive deals related to health. Therefore, it is essential to establish your brand and not restrict and try to have a diverse audience.

Moreover, it is necessary to identify the kind of traffic that you draw to your Triller account. Most people make content that kids generally liked, whereas some make content that young adults and kids enjoy. If you are aware of the audience's demographic that you attract, you can confidently pitch to different brands about why they should promote their product to your audience.

Moreover, one should not be ashamed of reaching out to companies to get paid promotion deals. Instead of waiting for them to discover you amidst thousands of other creators, reaching out to them can earn you a gig and a lucrative deal. Landing a deal will be easier if you approach brands that are currently sponsoring other creators with a similar audience to yours on the platform. Additionally, do not be demotivated if you start small since you are always going to climb up and build your portfolio to attract more prominent brands. To approach the firm, use your Triller account to directly message (DM) them. Brands usually maintain a social media presence, especially on platforms that they are promoting their product. Doing so will allow them to easily access your profile and decide if you would be the right choice. Additionally, always have your contact information, preferably your formal email address, in your Bio. This will make it easier for brands to contact you for potential brand deals.

It is also very important that you know what your brand is worth, meaning you should know how much you will charge the brands if you get a promotion deal. This depends on the number of followers you have and the number of likes your average post receives. One cent for every follower is considered an average in the social media industry, but you do not need to stick to this figure. You can negotiate the terms to make the brand pay you more. Never highball as it will scare brands away, and never understate the offer as you will not be fairly compensated.

Choose the products and services that you promote on your Triller accounts very wisely. Only promote things that you personally would use or consider are worth the money. Although many creators have confessed promoting products despite their personal opinion being that the products are not worth it, you can lose your fans' trust by doing so. The loyalty and trust of your fans need to be preserved under all circumstances as they define your success on the platform.

OTHER MODES OF MAKING MONEY

Social media is a vast platform and has countless opportunities to be benefitted from. Since most of the world is now on social media, people have found various ways to make money on these platforms. Some of these much lesser-known and unique ways in which one can make money are discussed below.

Lesser-Known Ways to Make Money

It is rumored that followers and likes in the future will become a commodity, and value will be attached to them like real money. This is already becoming a reality as people are paying well-established account owners to buy their profiles. More likes and followers means that you have a higher social standing than others with lower social figures. Teenagers to adults, everyone well-familiar with technology, are obsessed with social media, and this is why such activities have been happening on Instagram and also TikTok. Similarly, Triller also offers the opportunity for you to do the same. It is early enough to get in on the ground game in this platform.

Decide a niche for your Triller profile, be it food, fitness, lifestyle, or post content related to the niche. Cleverly decide the niche, as you cannot attach your face to the profile, and it has to be worthy enough for brands to invest in. Food-related accounts are often seen making short clips of dishes served at restaurants and present it aesthetically. Such niches have an insane amount of following and are reached out to by brands in the food industry, which is a billion-dollar industry, to promote their product. Once you have amassed a decent following, you can sell to interested people. Using your Triller bio, you can attract such people to the account, hold life on this medium, or others to announce that you are selling it or auction it there. The higher the number of followers you have, the higher will be the amount you get in return to let go of the account.

Moreover, celebrities and other influencers who have a lot on their plate cannot be directly responsible for their accounts and often lookout for people with experience to run their accounts. Companies also look for experienced people to run their social media pages, and you might have heard about the 'social media teams.' If you have a generous number of followers on your Triller account, can caption your posts well, have a way with words, or simply have a library of Triller ideas, people will employ you. People need someone responsible who has experience in coordinating and running social media campaigns. There are marketing agencies that have a social media sector dedicated to this with many experts. You can reach out to brands, firms, businesses, influencers that you think might need your help and offer them your services. This mode of making money might be challenging but not impossible. Since Triller is just now coming to the forefront, your knowledge will be more coveted than people familiar with the established platforms.

As discussed above, fans are willing to pay many dollars to meet their celebrities or to have any kind of personal interaction with them. Depending on your talent and social media following, you can charge money to meet your fans or perform for them. Celebrities who perform at events charge money, and when we say the money, we mean mad cash. Similarly, if you have a following, you can be paid thousands of dollars to attend a party, attend an opening ceremony, perform at an event, or even record a video message for someone. Although some might find themselves in a moral dilemma to charge people who love them to meet, it is not unknown that various YouTubers have held a meet and greets with tickets valued at hundreds if not thousands of dollars.

You can start a virtual shop on Triller. Instagram shops might not be something that you might be unfamiliar with, and even some of the people you know might be running their business on these platforms. Since Triller is fundamentally a similar platform, starting an online shop is possible. You can make Triller clips of the products you are selling. If it is an apparel store, you can model it; if it is a furniture store, you can display it; if it is a toy store, you can play with it; the possibilities are endless. Triller's advantage is that you can make it fun, reach out to people that you might not have thought of, and boost your sales. This platform's trending nature has the potential of breaking charts for a toy or clothing that is unique. Think of the countless purchases you might have made through something you saw on TikTok, Facebook, or Instagram. So, if you have an entrepreneurial mind and are willing to make an effort, starting a virtual shop might be for you.

Unconventional Ways of Making Money

Sometimes social media can be a weird space, and you may find people selling products and services that are too bizarre. The following methods are not advised to be employed to make money on Triller. However, one may note that if they want, they can cash money through such opportunities.

Switching platforms after you have amassed a considerable following and popularity is very common. People who start on social media switch to professional singing, modeling, acting, or form their own business. The fame and recognition that one gets can make it possible. Although this method does not allow you to make money on Triller, it is possible to make money through Triller. If you are known on the app for lip-syncing, you might find yourself getting offers for minor or major roles in TV shows and movies. If you are known for making random clips and have interacting content, you might receive an offer for a podcast or a reality show.

Similarly, if you are known for food, you might get your very own cooking show on the television. These things have happened in the past and can occur through Triller. It would be best if you employed an agent who can make this all possible and have contact in the respective industries. Although this method is not completely rare, it is rather unconventional for social media stars to leave the platform altogether.

One bizarre way to earn money, if you have an immense and loyal following, is to auction some of your personal belongings. If you are active socially and a Shane Dawson fan, you might be aware of the incident where he listed his used underwear on eBay and received the highest bid of 100,000 dollars. No one is asking you to sell your used underwear, but other used clothing items, personal belongings like a toy that is repeatedly used in your Triller videos, an autographed object can do well amongst fans. However, you need to draw the line where you are exploiting your fans or giving them a piece of you to show them your appreciation. Fans can identify any exploitation, and this can result in you losing followers, which you worked extremely hard to earn.

Every content creator should be mindful of the consequences and their audience's perception before employing any of the above methods to earn fast money. Nowadays, there is no room for making mistakes on social media, as you are answerable to an army of fans, and the consequences, as a result, are ten folds of what they would be in real life.

CONCLUSION

These were some of the many methods that are practiced by social media influencers around the world, and that can be mimicked on Triller. However, social media platforms are too big, and the opportunities available are infinite. People every day are coming up with innovative ways to use their social media presence to earn money. Triller is also similar. With time, the application will only grow, and so will the opportunities to earn cash for its users. Until then, this book, by running through the application itself and by discussing methods to generate money, has provided you with ample guidelines to start your own Triller account and take advantage of the various financial opportunities available.

It is important to note that the working of the mentioned methods is highly dependent on your audience and the geographical region from which you are based. It is crucial that one does not take this book's recommendations as a hard fact, as running a successful brand is about adapting. Learn from the teachings of this book, alter it to impact your situation favorably, and multiply your revenue.

Lastly, challenge yourself and think outside of the box because people on Triller, like any other social media application, like something different and charismatic. As long you hold on these principles, you are set to make 'mad cash' on Triller.

And finally, if you liked the book, I would like to ask you to do me a favor and leave a review for the book on Amazon. This book is intentionally short so that it fits under the quick read category, but I would love to expand it if there is interest. Let me know in the review if you want this book to be longer or to include any additional information.

Type in this website to leave a review.

http://mybook.to/Triller

If you want a free copy of my next book, please sign up to be on my VIP list. Here is the website:

https://www.subscribepage.com/getafreebook

Thank you, and good luck!

Made in the USA
Middletown, DE
20 September 2020